Old KIMBERLEY

by
David Ottewell

A panoramic view of Kimberley taken from the mortuary chapel. Cemetery Road is in the foreground, leading past the United Methodist Free Church to Main Street. The open space between Noel Street (on the right) and Newdigate Street (to the left) is the site of Kimberley Institute cricket ground, a venue for many celebratory gatherings. When the photograph was taken houses had only been built on one side of Newdigate Street. Cloverlands, the large house built for the Hanson family in the 1890s, can just be seen in the distance. It was demolished in 1967.

© David Ottewell 2001
First published in the United Kingdom, 2001,
by Stenlake Publishing
Telephone / Fax: 01290 551122

ISBN 1 84033 155 0

FURTHER READING

The books listed below were used by the author during his
research. None of them are available from Stenlake Publishing.
Those interested in finding out more are advised to contact their
local bookshop or reference library.

H. Mather, *The Story of Kimberley*, 1957.
A. Plumb, *Kimberley in Old Postcards*, vols. 1–6, European Library,
  1988–1993.
R. Baron Von Hube, *Griseleia in Snotinghscire*, Nottingham Book
  Co., 1901.

Brothers William and Thomas Hardy originally operated a
wholesale beer business in nearby Heanor. In 1857 they decided
to move to Kimberley and take up the manufacturing of beer,
buying out the established business belonging to Samuel
Robinson. In 1861 they moved 200 yards to a new site where
Robert Grace of Burton on Trent had designed them a new
brewery, illustrated here. This was extended in 1882 to cope with
increased business. The Kimberley Brewery still employs a
number of local people today.

INTRODUCTION

Kimberley lies six miles to the north-west of Nottingham and two miles from the border of the neighbouring county of Derbyshire.

Little is known about the town's early history, though it is referred to in the Domesday Book (1086) by the name Chinmarelie. It began to be spelt with a K from about 1200 and the spelling Kimberley was first used in the fifteenth century, although this did not become standardised until the end of the sixteenth century. The Domesday Book records that there were two manors in the area, as well as one farmhouse and two cottages. For taxation purposes the area was assessed as comprising three and a half carucates (roughly 420 acres), plus a wood four furlongs by two. William the Conqueror gave the lands of Kimberley to one of his followers, William de Peverel.

It is difficult to date the first church in Kimberley: a picture in a book produced in 1790 suggests a twelfth century origin while the first record of a rector does not appear until the end of the thirteenth century. What is sure is that the church stood on Grangers Hill (the area at the top of Factory Lane going towards Swingate). The house belonging to the lord of the manor was also in this area.

Kimberley was originally a small farming community little affecting, or affected by, other villages or towns in the area. Indeed in 1428 it was found that the village had less than ten householders and as a result the parish was combined with that of nearby Greasley.

Visitors to Kimberley in the eighteenth century found the church to be in ruins. Like many other rural communities, however, Kimberley saw an upsurge in its fortunes in the late eighteenth to early nineteenth centuries when the country became more industrialised. One sign of this was the expansion of the railways, another the opening of coal mines. By 1840 it was noted that 1,778 people lived in the Kimberley area.

The people of Kimberley had their own cottage industries such as framework knitting, used to produce hosiery, and as the nineteenth century progressed Victorian entrepreneurs set up companies manufacturing beer, leather and lace, which provided employment for locals and attracted many more to live in the area. This led to a spate of housebuilding to accommodate workers, and the development of community facilities such as shops, schools, churches and chapels.

Improved communications aided the development of Kimberley and district. In the 1760s the turnpike road opened, and in the 1870s two railway lines arrived in the town. A passenger service on the Great Northern Railway's Nottingham and Erewash Valley line commenced on 1 August 1876, while on 12 August 1879 the Midland Railway Company opened a second station in the town. The final piece of transport infrastructure was put in place on 1 January 1914 when the fifteen mile Notts. and Derbyshire Tramways Company route between Ripley and Nottingham was opened fully. This passed through Kimberley and was affectionately known as the 'Ripley Rattler'.

No. 3.

The Stag Inn, situated at the brow of the hill on the main road into Kimberley from Nottingham, can trace its origins to the early years of the eighteenth century when it was located in one of a row of four cottages. When this photograph was taken E. Bostock was the landlord. The horse is pulling a water cart belonging to Arthur Clay of Manor Farm. The present Stag Inn is set behind the range of buildings pictured here.

Knowle, Kimberley, Notts.

Photo Series.

This surprisingly rural scene was taken on the main road to Nottingham. One of Kimberley's two blacksmiths operated from the premises on the left. The three pairs of semi-detached houses in the distance on the right remain today, while the wall just before them borders the garden of Sidney House.

THE KNOWLE KIMBERLEY

PEVERIL SERIES

Kimberley had two toll bars on the turnpike road that ran through the village, one at Chapel Bar and the other in this vicinity at Knowle Hill. It remained in place from the 1760s until its removal in 1876. From here the road now descends into the centre of Kimberley, although originally the Nuthall road swung left taking the traveller towards Swingate and thence on to High Street.

Kimberley Colliery was based in the area known today as Swingate. It was opened in 1852 by local entrepreneur Thomas North, who also had pits at Babbington, Newthorpe, Strelley and Awsworth. Soon afterwards a railway was built to link Kimberley pit with the colliery at Cinderhill, and a stationary steam engine was placed close to Kimberley pit to draw the wagons uphill from Cinderhill. The mine did not have a particularly long life and ceased producing coal in 1897, although it continued to be used for water pumping. In 1974 a slippage of soil caused an old shaft from the colliery to appear suddenly in a front garden in Clive Crescent, a reminder of earlier days.

HIGH St KIMBERLEY. (NOTTS) 288-15.

High Street is very much a backwater of Kimberley today, but in times past this was the centre of the village and the main road through it. The original church and manor house were located in this area. The Highland Laddie, the public house to the left, has now been demolished.

By the middle of the nineteenth century it had become obvious that Kimberley needed a new burial ground and a suitable site was sought. Earl Cowper, the largest landowner in the area, offered a seven-and-a-half acre site on a hill close to the Knowle. This was readily accepted and Richard Charles Sutton of Nottingham was charged with the task of designing and building a mortuary chapel and laying out the grounds. £2,700 was spent on the project, which was completed in November 1883. The first burial in the new cemetery, that of a child, took place on 10 November 1883. Access to the site was through a set of ornate iron gates at the top of Cemetery Road (renamed Broomhill Road in 1938). The distinctive bell turret on the chapel was removed in the 1950s when it was considered to be in danger of falling down.

Richard Sutton of Nottingham, who had shown his proficiency when designing the cemetery and mortuary chapel in 1883, was again employed to oversee the building of the United Methodist Free Church. This project, on a site at the junction of Cemetery Road and Main Street, was undertaken in 1890. The land cost £150 and £2,650 was spent on the building. Local stone was used in the construction and the church organist, William Donelly, supplied much of the internal joinery (see the picture on page 20, which features a number of William Donelly's employees).

NOEL STREET KIMBERLEY.

The terraced houses of Noel Street were built at the end of the nineteenth century to provide accommodation for the influx of workers to Kimberley in the latter years of Queen Victoria's reign, many of whom were employed in Victoria Mills. It took its name from Noel Birkin, a member of the family who owned the lace factory at the time. Flanking Noel Street on Main Street were two pairs of semi-detached houses which were built at the same time. Being of better quality than their counterparts on Noel Street, these were reserved for the senior staff at the Birkin lace factory.

MAIN ST.
KIMBERLEY

Prominent Nottingham lace manufacturer Richard Birkin probably decided to set up a branch of his company in Kimberley because land prices were more reasonable than in the centre of Nottingham and there was a plentiful supply of cheap labour. On 24 March 1880 Mrs Birkin laid the foundation stone for the new factory on Main Street. It was to be called Victoria Mills. Builders Shaw and Co. of Kimberley worked quickly, for the factory was opened less than three months later on 12 June 1880. The large building, which employed many local people, dominated the scene in Kimberley for many years. For some time the factory was operated by the Kimberley Lace Company. Eventually, with a falling off in demand for lace the factory was sold and Wolsey Ltd. took over. They prospered and added extensions of their own, producing quality hosiery. Ultimately the competition from cheap imports led to Wolsey closing. Demolition followed in 1983 after which the sites of their factories were redeveloped as shopping complexes.

A 1930s' view of Main Street showing the changes made to the Lord Clyde pub in the twenty years since the picture on the inside front cover was taken. Here it boasts bay windows on the ground floor and a raised entrance. The advertisement for Player's Navy Cut tobacco and cigarettes has local connections, for many people in this area worked at the extensive Player's factories in Nottingham. A little further down the street can be seen the YMCA building, opened in 1908 and known as Hardy House. Today this is the site of the library. The picture can be dated to after April 1933 because there are no tram tracks and the trolleybus wires are in position. Trolleybuses took over from trams on the Ripley to Nottingham route on 25 April 1933.

Kimberley: Nottingham Road. *Rex Series. No. 1402.*

Main Street photographed from the opposite direction to the previous picture and about ten years earlier. This was a junction point where the track doubled to allow trams to pass each other – the line was single track for most of its length. The post outside the Lord Clyde marked a stopping point. The ornate war memorial stands on the corner of Factory Lane facing Victoria Street.

Like all other communities in Britain, big and small, Kimberley wanted to recognise those local men who had given their lives in the First World War. A fund was started and £1,500 of the sum raised was used to build the war memorial, commemorating 54 local men who died in the conflict. It was unveiled in front of a large crowd by the Rev. Frederick Hart in 1921. Rev. Hart had a big influence on the life of Kimberley, serving as rector for 42 years from July 1890 to March 1932. Note the headstocks of Kimberley pit, by this time redundant, on the hill in the background.

The overspill of the crowd at the unveiling of the war memorial in 1921 fills the space at the junction of Factory Lane and Main Street. The entrance to Victoria Mills is to the right. Close scrutiny of the photograph shows that a band is playing and the crowd singing as they congregate around banners from local Methodist churches.

MAIN STREET
KIMBERLEY.

The further-away section of Main Street visible in this picture, looking towards Newdigate Street, remains populated by shops, although naturally the businesses have changed somewhat over the years. Nearer to the camera the Primitive Methodist Chapel, which opened in 1876 with seating for 608, closed in 1962. After being used as a supermarket for a period it is now a theme bar. The Sunday school room was demolished and the space at present acts as a car park.

Main Street, Kimberley.

This photograph can be dated to some time between 1914 and 1918 for on the wall of Chapel Bar, facing Newdigate Street, is a poster appealing to the patriotism of locals: 'Volunteer Now in Your Country's Hour of Need'. Other signs mention the Bantam Battalion and the Field Artillery. The third shop along is H. Green and Sons chemists, prominently advertising enemas! The newsagents next door offers a collection service both for parcels and the Junction Laundry.

Main Street, Kimberley, Notts.

Peveril series 4141

Kimberley was on the Notts. and Derbyshire Tramways Company route between Ripley in Derbyshire and Nottingham. The fifteen mile route, which opened fully on 1 January 1914, was claimed to be the most dangerous in the British Isles owning to its length and the gradient involved. Two different types of tram operated on the system. The first was the open-topped variety, such as this example pictured on Main Street. Another dozen covered trams were also ordered and proved more popular. The trams had a livery of light green and cream with gold lining. They ran until 5 October 1932 and the following year a trolleybus service began operating on the route.

The Main Street through Kimberley from Nottingham to Eastwood and beyond, seen from near the junction with James Street. The men in aprons have taken time out from their work at William Donelly & Sons joinery works on Rockside to pose for the photographer. In the middle distance is the Great Northern Hotel. The level crossing gate is closed across Station Road while a train waits at the Great Northern station.

Taken from the corner of James Street, this photograph captures a horse-drawn delivery van belonging to local baker Ernest Blanchard. Mr Blanchard had premises at No. 6 James Street; previously he had had a shop in Ilkeston. The business prospered and after the Second World War the company moved to a large bakery at Watnall. Behind the delivery van is the row known as Chapel Bar, which led down to Station Road and has sadly been demolished.

Kimberley: Main Street.

Rex Series No. 1401.

A similar view to the previous picture but taken about fifteen years later. The Queen's Head Inn (whose licensee was Sarah Pierson at the time), has a tramcar stopping point opposite, and the former shop at the Newdigate Street end of Chapel Bar has been converted to a sub branch of Barclays Bank. The main branch was at nearby Eastwood.

An unidentified gathering at Chapel Bar Toll featured on a postcard sent from the town on 12 August 1908. The white gate sign to the left advertises the Gate Inn. It would have taken its name from the ancient barrier that stood across the road when this was a turnpike road on which tolls were levied.

Many Sunday school demonstrations (as these processions were known) began at the Great Northern station and made their way up Station Road to the centre of Kimberley. The Great Northern Hotel, in the background, was built when the station was constructed in the 1870s. Sadly it burnt down during the Second World War. The metal bridge carried the Great Northern railway lines over the main road and has also now been removed.

During the first half of the twentieth century when attendances at the local Methodist chapels were high, joint social gatherings were often arranged. Here a procession is wending its way up Station Road with a crowd gathered on either side of the road to watch it pass. The corner of The Firs (see page 27) and its garden can be seen across Main Street. The two shops in view are those of plumber William Nix and Jas. Nelson and Sons Ltd.

STATION ROAD
KIMBERLEY

Station Road and Main Street photographed from the Great Northern Hotel, with the railway bridge in the foreground. The station yard lies off to the left, and the Cricketers Rest pub can be seen in the distance. Previously it was known as the Mason's Arms. Despite being in the heartland of the Hardy and Hanson breweries it is advertising Stretton's fine Derby ales.

THE FIRS

The Firs has an interesting history, having been built in 1874 by the Great Northern Railway Company as a form of payment to the brewer William Hardy. In exchange he signed some land and a row of three terraced houses over to the railway company. The Firs included stables, a coach house and hayloft, and is believed to have been designed by the famous Nottingham architect T. C. Hine. In the early years of the twentieth century (c.1910) The Firs was owned by William Oldershaw, a manufacturing chemist. It was purchased by the Digby Colliery (see page 47) in 1925 to house their colliery manager, Edward Stoker Fawcett, and in 1938 Ernest Blanchard, of bakery fame, bought it. As well as being a family home, it also served a number of other functions including housing a nursery school and an old people's home. In 1986 it fell into the hands of developers, and, much to the anger of local people, was demolished in June 1988. One of the most interesting feature of The Firs, and its only remaining relic, is a stained glass window depicting a scene entitled 'The Four Ages of Man', which now has pride of place in the parish hall. This was made about 1862 by Heaton, Turnill, Bayne of London, probably for the school on Chapelside. The school was demolished in the 1870s after which the window was rescued and found its way to The Firs.

NEWDIGATE St KIMBERLEY. 288-10.

When the two railway lines were being built through Kimberley in the 1870s, their promoters wished to set up operations in the most advantageous locations in the town, and demolished and moved two schools in order to do so. In 1879 the Midland Railway acquired and knocked down the National School, building a replacement on Church Hill. Earlier, in 1873–1874, the Great Northern Railway had agreed to build a replacement British School (its distinctive gable end can be seen on the left of this picture of Newdigate Street), in exchange for being allowed to demolish the old school on Station Road. The schoolmaster's house, built at the same time, can just be seen beyond the school.

Many boys received their education at the British School in Newdigate Street until it was superseded by the County Secondary School, which opened in purpose-built premises further up the street in 1946. This school group dates from 1910.

For many years the school's headmaster was Albert S. Langton. The serried ranks of desks in this picture of a classroom at the British School suggest a very formal style of teaching.

Kimberley celebrated the Coronation of King George V and Queen Mary on Thursday 22 June 1911 in a burst of patriotic fervour. Mrs Mary Ann Hanson of Cloverlands planted an oak tree on the corner of Factory Lane, near where the war memorial was to be erected ten years later, and in the afternoon groups processed to the cricket ground from their various churches and chapels. At 2.30 p.m., headed by the Bulwell Excelsior Prize Band, they left the cricket ground in a procession that passed along Victoria Street, Factory Lane, High Street, James Street, Main Street and back to Factory Lane for singing. All those who took part received a Coronation medal, and the younger children were given small flags. After celebration teas the day was rounded off at 10.00 p.m. with the lighting of a bonfire on Pit Hill.

Kimberley was bedecked with flags, pictures and bunting for the Coronation day celebrations in 1911. This picture shows part of the procession near Chapel Bar. Programmes listing the days events were printed and distributed, and included hymn sheets for songs to be sung at the rallying points of the Institute cricket ground and Factory Lane.

Newdigate Street led to the village of Watnall and was normally a quiet thoroughfare, although the Institute cricket ground, off to the left, attracted crowds on special occasions (see page 30). In the far distance on the right the gable end of the British School can be seen.

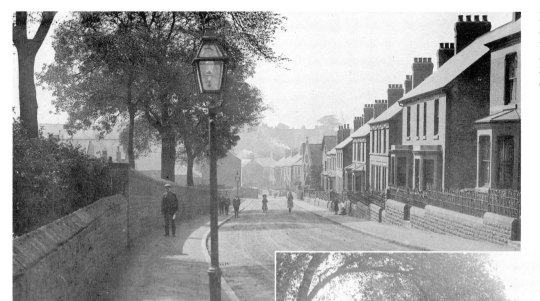

The citizens of Kimberley out in force to witness King George V and Queen Mary driving through the town on 25 June 1914. The royal couple were on their way to Ilkeston via Kimberley, Eastwood and Heanor.

Dr George Ross Northwood was a respected doctor in Kimberley for many years. He lived on Victoria Street and later at the bottom of Newdigate Street where the car park is today. Initially he visited his patients in his horse and trap, although later he acquired a motor car. The vertical picture shows him in Norman Street, while in the second view he is standing proudly by his car at the gates to Cloverlands, the Hanson family home. At one time Dr Northwood was president of the Kimberley Institute Cricket Club.

Information on the reverse of this picture reveals that it shows the Kimberley Co-op in James Street in 1936. The names given are James Williamson, Percy Jeffries, Abe Shaw and Edwin Turton. The co-op had premises on both sides of James Street, and in more recent times (*c.*1967) operated from a two-storey shop on Main Street.

Like many small communities in the era before television, Kimberley had its own cinema. The Town Picture Palace was situated on Regent Street and opened in August 1912. In 1919 a fire caused a lot of damage and necessitated extensive rebuilding. The newly repaired cinema proved extremely popular and soon could not cope with demand, so in 1929 a second storey which included a balcony was added. The owners took the opportunity to rename it the Regent Cinema at the same time. The building saw its last days as a cinema in 1957 and later opened as a supermarket and then a billiard hall.

A church is first mentioned in Kimberley in 1298, although there is likely to have been one prior to that date. By the end of the eighteenth century the old church, which was situated on Granger Hill, was in ruins and parishioners had to travel to Greasley church for services. The desperate need for a new church in Kimberley was met in 1847 when the present church was built using Bulwell stone. It cost £2,300 and had seating for 521. Initially it shared a rector with Greasley church, but on 22 October 1852 William St George Sargent was installed as the first rector of Kimberley. In this picture the bell tower has a wooden casing behind it. This was temporary housing for the eight tubular bells which were fitted in the church on 9 August 1902 to commemorate the Coronation of Edward VII.

The rectory in Kimberley was built in 1852, the same year as the first rector was appointed. £1,100 was spent on its construction, but its facilities were apparently not adequate as in 1872 the then incumbent spent £700 adding an extra wing and an entrance porch. The rectory served the parish until 1967 when it was demolished. A new rectory was built in 1971.

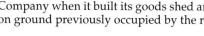

The area of Kimberley by the parish church and rectory is intriguingly known as 'Nine Corners'. A visit to the area and a count of the corners fails to provide nine, leaving the question of the derivation of the name. Some have advanced the theory that nine elms once stood at this point, and that the name started out as Nine Elms Corner and became corrupted over the years.

This picture was taken a little further back up Eastwood Road, and shows the sharp bend created in the 1870s by the Midland Railway Company when it built its goods shed and yard on ground previously occupied by the road.

MIDLAND STATION, KIMBERLEY NOTTS.

In 1879 the Midland Railway Company opened a branch line through Kimberley to connect with the main lines at Basford Junction and Bennerley Junction. The station was designed by the company's engineer, Charles Trubshaw, and was built by a Derby firm at a cost of £2,495. It opened on 12 August 1879. A passenger service continued until 1917 at which time the line from Kimberley to Bennerley was taken up and scrapped during a First World War economy drive. The line from Kimberley to Nottingham continued to be used by goods services until 1950.

HARDY'S BREWERY. KIMBERLEY.

There has been a Kimberley brewery since 1832 when Samuel Robinson established one in a converted bakehouse. In 1847 Stephen Hanson, the farm manager at Nuthall Temple Estate, moved to Kimberley and set up in competition with Robinson. Ten years later Samuel Robinson sold out to the Hardy brothers and the rivalry between the Hardys and Hanson began. The quality of the water, drawn from a natural spring called Alley Spring, contributed to the brewing of good ale. As time wore on competition from other companies became fierce, and in 1930 it was decided to merge the two Kimberley companies, although they continued to trade separately until 1951. The famous Hardys and Hansons Kimberley ales remain the favoured drink of many local people today.

40

A train passing through the Great Northern Railway's station in Kimberley. The bridge in the background provided pedestrian access between up and down platforms. A Nottingham to Derby passenger service via Kimberley commenced in 1876 and finally ceased in September 1964, although the bridge carrying the line over Main Street wasn't demolished until March 1971.

Kimberley Viaduct.
Pax Photo 1408

Work began on the viaduct at Kimberley in 1871. It was a major undertaking, with a span of 40 arches over a length of 1,760 feet, and drew many itinerant construction workers to the area. It is said that some of the navvies lived in the bricked up arches of the viaduct as they worked on its construction. The Great Northern Railway opened the viaduct to goods trains in September 1875 and the first passenger service crossed it on 1 August 1876. The line was known as the Nottingham and Erewash Valley line, and soon there were nine trains each way daily, with eleven on Saturdays and three on Sundays running to Pinxton.

This view of Eastwood Road dates to before 1913 when tramlines were laid and it became part of the route of the Ripley Rattler. Eastwood Road leads up towards Gilthill.

A section of Eastwood Road at the bottom of Maws Lane. This area was known as New Kimberley and was developed in the final years of the nineteenth century. Queen Victoria celebrated her Diamond Jubilee in 1897 and this event gave rise to another name for the area, Jubilee. When the picture was taken the corner shop belonged to G. W. Jackson, grocer.

Maws Lane branches off Eastwood Road beside G. Jackson's former grocers shop (featured on the previous page). Construction of the houses on the left commenced in 1897, while those visible across the top of the road are in Edinburgh Row. The photograph clearly illustrates the rising ground here and it was in the area to the left of Maws Lane that Kimberley's windmills were situated.

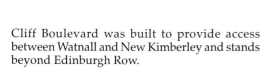

Cliff Boulevard was built to provide access between Watnall and New Kimberley and stands beyond Edinburgh Row.

The Old Mill, Kimberley, Notts. Highest Point in the County.   Peveril Series. 527.

'The Lawns' was a piece of high ground on which Kimberley's windmills were located from the start of the nineteenth century and possibly earlier. In 1837 William Widdowson moved from Strelley Mill to take over operations at Kimberley. Eventually he decided to expand his milling and bought one of a row of mills that stood by the side of the forest in Nottingham. He had this transferred to Kimberley, and afterwards also built a steam mill at the Lawns. In 1865 the East Mill burnt down but the West Mill, seen here, continued in operation until January 1883 when a gale blew off the sails, which were not replaced. The building fell into disuse and much of its stonework was broken up and taken away to use in other building projects in the locality.

DIGBY COLLIERY, KIMBERLEY, NOTTS.

The Digby Colliery at the Giltbrook end of Kimberley was sunk in 1866, just a year before the nearby New London Colliery. There were branch lines linking them to the nearby Midland Railway. By the 1930s both pits were considered to be uneconomic to continue and they were closed on 5 November 1937.

Kimberley Viaduct.
Pex Photo. 1409

The Giltbrook end of the Kimberley viaduct. The Gate Inn has a prominent advertisement for locally-brewed Hardys ale. The viaduct, known affectionately as the Forty Arches, was eventually demolished in 1973, and the final arch to be left standing was the one spanning the road.